Seeds of a Nation

STATE OF OREGON

1859

Oregon

P.M. Boekhoff and Stuart A. Kallen

KIDHAVEN PRESS™

THOMSON

GALE

© 2004 by KidHaven Press. KidHaven Press is an imprint of The Gale Group, Inc., a division of Thomson Learning, Inc.

KidHaven™ and Thomson Learning™ are trademarks used herein under license.

For more information, contact
KidHaven Press
27500 Drake Rd.
Farmington Hills, MI 48331-3535
Or you can visit our Internet site at http://www.gale.com

LIBRARY OF CONGRESS CATALOGING-IN-PUBLICATION DATA

Boekhoff, P. M. (Patti Marlene), 1957–
  Oregon / by P.M. Boekhoff and Stuart A. Kallen
    p. cm. — (Seeds of a nation)
   Summary: Discusses the early history of Oregon beginning with the Native Americans who lived there for many years, through European exploration and settlement, to statehood in 1859.
   Includes bibliographical references (p.) and index.
   ISBN 0-7377-1482-4 (hardback : alk. paper)
   1. Oregon—History—Juvenile literature   [1. Oregon History.]
I. Kallen, Stuart A., 1955– . II. Title. III. Series.
F876.3.B64 2004
979.5-dc21

                                                            200215518

Printed in the United States of America

Contents

Chapter One

The Native Americans

Oregon is home to nearly 3 million people and is known for its rugged Pacific coast, salmon-filled rivers, and sky-scraping, snowcapped mountains. The state is located in the northwest corner of the United States between Washington to the north, Idaho to the east, California and Nevada to the south, and the Pacific Ocean to the west.

Long before Oregon became the tenth-largest state in America, it was inhabited by about one hundred Native American tribes. These included the Clatsop, Klamath, Walla Walla, Umpqua, and Tillamook. Their lives and cultures were as rich and varied as the natural environments in which they lived.

Each of these tribes had its own language. Yet all of the people in this region also spoke the language of the

Chinook, a tribe of great traders known to all the people of Oregon. Using the Chinook language, people from different tribes met socially and traded with one another.

The Coastal Clatsop

The coastal people of Oregon, such as the Clatsop and the Tillamook, lived along the Pacific Ocean in forests of red cedar, spruce, and fir. In this foggy, wet region about seventy five inches of rain falls every year, and it can rain every day for weeks at a time.

The Clatsop tribe lived on the northwest tip of Oregon, along the Columbia River and the Pacific shores. They were builders and navigators, skilled hunters and fishermen. They were also expert traders, **bartering** goods with many other tribes in the area.

Oregon's Place in the United States Today

The Clatsop built homes, called earth lodges, from cedar planks cut from trees. To do this, they used tools made from sharpened stones and seashells. Their homes were very large, holding as many as one hundred people under a single roof. To build the houses, they dug a deep rectangular pit and built up a ledge of earth around it. The floor and walls were lined with planks. Only the triangle-shaped roof showed above ground. Such houses, called pit houses or earth shelters, are cooler in summer and warmer in winter than above-ground houses.

The Clatsop used cedar for many other purposes. They even made soft, velvety, rain-resistant clothing from the bark. To make such clothing, Clatsop women stripped cedar bark from the trees, shredded it, and wove it into fabric for skirts, capes, hats, and other items. They only wore such clothing in the coldest weather. Other times, they wore no clothing, painting their bodies with red dye and decorating themselves with shells, feathers, and animal fur.

Fishing and Trading

The Clatsop lived on clams, crabs, oysters, nuts, and wild fruit such as blackberries, but their most valued food was salmon. When the pink and silver king salmon made their yearly migration up the Columbia River, tribe members used nets, traps, hooks, and spears to catch tens of thousands of the fish. Another desirable catch was smelt, which contained so much fish oil that it could be lit on fire and used like candles, earning it the name candlefish.

Native Americans of Oregon use nets, hooks, and spears to catch salmon in the Columbia River.

Fishing continued through the summer and fall. The catch was divided evenly among the people by spiritual leaders called shamans. Uneaten fish were smoked over fires or dried in the sun.

The extra fish were loaded into canoes by Clatsop traders who paddled up the Columbia River every summer to barter with tribes that lived inland. They traded salmon, seashells, and other goods from the coast for things such as stone tools, buffalo skins, and tobacco.

The Klamath Tribe

Southwest of the Clatsop homeland lived several thousand members of the Klamath tribe. They made their homes in the Klamath River basin, a small, fertile river valley between the Coast mountain ranges to the west and the Cascade Range to the east. Within this basin is Klamath **marsh**, along with many lakes and rivers.

These bodies of water provided an endless supply of fish and pond-lily seeds which the tribes called *wokas*. Women in canoes harvested these seeds every August and September. Sometimes the Klamath ate the raw seeds. Often, the *wokas* were dried, ground

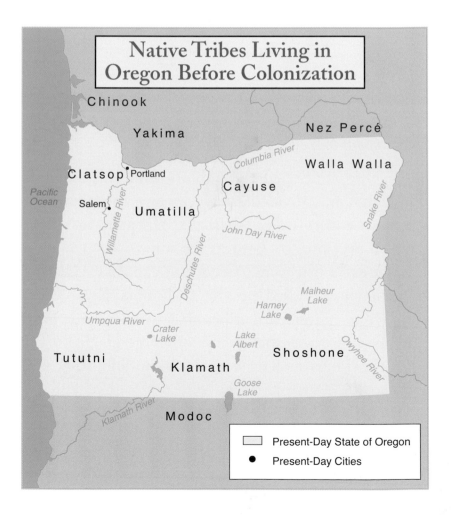

Native Tribes Living in Oregon Before Colonization

Chinook

Yakima

Nez Percé

Clatsop Portland

Columbia River

Walla Walla

Pacific Ocean

Cayuse

Salem

Willamette River

Umatilla

John Day River

Snake River

Deschutes River

Umpqua River

Malheur Lake

Harney Lake

Crater Lake

Lake Albert

Shoshone

Owyhee River

Tututni

Klamath

Goose Lake

Klamath River

Modoc

☐ Present-Day State of Oregon

● Present-Day Cities

into flour, and baked into flatbread or were cooked into porridge. These foods were also stored for use during the winter.

The Klamath lived in permanent villages in the winter. At the end of the cold season, when the ground began to thaw, the Klamath left their earth lodges. They spent spring, summer, and fall camping near the best fishing and hunting sites. These special areas were also favored for the fruits, vegetables, herbs, roots, flowers, and nuts that could be gathered nearby.

Fish provided an important food source and held spiritual meaning for the Klamath. They believed that gods and goddesses appeared in birds, fish, and other animals as well as in natural occurrences such as lightning, wind, and rain. Every year when the first sucker fish appeared, religious ceremonies were held as tribe members performed magic songs that they had heard in their dreams. Such rituals were followed by feasting, dancing, and celebration.

The People of the Columbia Plateau

Like the Klamath, tribes living east of the Cascade mountains were strongly influenced by the natural features of their homeland. These tribes included the Shoshone, Nez Percé, Walla Walla, Yakima, Paiute, and others.

In sunny eastern Oregon, rivers run through the canyons and grasslands of a flat high-desert region known as the Columbia plateau. Tribes used the mud, willows, and thin-leafed tule plants that grew near riverbeds to make longhouses. Measuring 20 to 150 feet long, each longhouse could hold four to eight families. These shelters consisted of poles tied together in an A-frame and covered with mats woven from tule plants. The clever design of these structures protected the Native Americans from searing heat, pouring rain, bone-chilling winds, and snow.

The plateau tribes traveled by foot over a large area throughout most of the year to find food in this dry, grassy region with few natural resources. In spring they visited the Columbia River to fish and trade with the Chinook. In early summer the tribes followed ancient trade routes to the foothills of the Blue Mountains to collect roots, seeds, nuts, leaves, and flowers for food and medicines. In late summer they climbed up the mountains to pick berries and hunt for antelope and bighorn sheep.

The Potlatch

In autumn, when the heavy rains began, fishing and trading ended. During this time people came from all over Oregon to gather along the Oregon coast. There, they celebrated their good fortune with potlatches. *Potlatch* is a Chinook word meaning "to give." Tribes throughout Oregon came together to give thanks by holding potlatches.

Potlatches were held to celebrate important family events such as weddings, births, coming-of-age ceremonies, or deaths. During a potlatch, hundreds of invited guests received gifts from their host.

The potlatches were so important that the hosts sometimes spent months, or even years, gathering

Shoshone women let their horses drink from a lake.

blankets, jewelry, statues, baskets, metal goods, masks, hats, and food for guests. In addition to gift giving, potlatches featured special costumes, dancing, singing, feasting, and religious rituals.

In this land of plenty, the people of Oregon lived in harmony with nature for thousands of years. And the wealth and beauty they preserved would soon bring thousands of explorers from all over the world.

Chapter Two

Explorers and Traders

I n the late 1500s, European explorers appeared along the Oregon coast. The visitors arrived in huge ships with billowing sails that the Native Americans called winged canoes. During this time period, Spanish explorers passed through the region, but they had little impact on the Chinook, Tillamook, and other tribes.

One of Great Britain's most famous explorers and pirates, Sir Francis Drake, also sailed up the coast of Oregon during the sixteenth century. Drake had recently raided Spanish warehouses in Panama, and his ship, the *Golden Hind*, was weighted down with tons of gold, silver, and jewels.

His daring robbery enraged the Spanish, who had filled their warehouses with goods they had taken from the Aztecs, Incas, and other native tribes of Central and

South America. The Spanish chased Drake, who sailed north in order to escape. By the time Drake reached the rugged Oregon coast, however, the *Golden Hind* was leaking badly. Drake sailed into a cove believed by some to be the present-day Whale Cove in Depoe Bay, Oregon. There, he spent thirty-six days repairing his ship.

Legends say that Drake's ship was so overloaded with loot that he had to bury about forty tons of his treasure around Whale Cove. Rumors of the treasure have inspired many voyagers to search for it over the centuries, although none have ever found it.

The pirate Sir Francis Drake sailed up the Oregon coast to escape capture.

Sir Francis Drake's ship, the Golden Hind, *held tons of stolen gold and jewels.*

Captain Cook

In 1778 British captain James Cook arrived in Oregon in search of another treasure—animal pelts. Cook found a churning sea, a dangerously rocky shore, and a pounding rainstorm with howling winds that almost put an end to his expedition. As Cook and his crew battled the elements, the captain saw cliffs towering five hundred feet above the sea. The captain named this rugged point of land Cape Foulweather after the fierce storm that surrounded him.

Cape Foulweather is the highest point along the Oregon coast. Native Americans often gathered there to look out over the crashing surf and watch whales swim across the horizon. In 1778 the Clatsop people also could see Captain Cook in his winged canoe.

When the storm cleared, the natives paddled out to sea in their canoes to trade with Captain Cook and his crew. They brought extremely valuable furs of bears, wolves, foxes, cougars, deer, raccoons, rabbits, seals, sea otters, and other animals to trade. In exchange, the natives received metal trinkets such as nails, files, knives, and a few brass buttons. Although these were worthless to the British, the Native Americans had rarely seen metal hardened and fashioned in this way, and so they greatly valued these objects.

Unfortunately, the Europeans brought more than iron and hardened metal tools. They also imported devastating diseases such as smallpox, measles, and cholera to the tribes.

Captain James Cook sailed to Oregon in search of animal pelts.

Because the native populations had never before been exposed to these illnesses, their bodies could not resist them, and thousands quickly died.

Gray Names the Columbia

In the years after Captain Cook's voyage, many European and American traders came for the valuable furs of Oregon. In 1788 American captain Robert Gray sailed from Boston with a shipful of brass buttons, blue cloth, beads, and other items to trade with the people of Tillamook Bay. After loading his ship with furs, Gray sailed on to China, where he traded the furs for silk, tea, and spices worth a thousand times more than he had paid for the pelts.

In 1792 Gray returned to Oregon again, looking for a mythical shortcut to China known as the Northwest Passage. Although such a passage does not exist, Gray thought he had found this route when he spotted a large river flowing into the Pacific. This river flows through a rocky area so dangerous and deadly that it is now known as the Graveyard of the Pacific because more than two hundred ships have wrecked there. Determined to find the Northwest Passage, Gray sailed toward it anyway. His ship was violently dashed about as he crossed through breaking waves and over one of the world's most dangerous sandbars.

Gray named the river Columbia in honor of his ship, the *Columbia Rediviva*. His crew stayed on the river and continued to trade with the Chinook until the cold winds of autumn began to blow. After selling his boatload of furs in China, Gray returned to Boston as a wealthy man. His success on the Columbia encouraged other American fur traders to stay on the river for long periods of time to barter with the natives of Oregon.

Lewis and Clark

Explorers continued to travel to Oregon by sea. But during the early nineteenth century, the first-known team of explorers traveled overland to the region.

Robert Gray, an American captain, named the Columbia River after his ship, the Columbia Rediviva.

Heading West

In 1803 the United States bought all of the land between the Mississippi River and the Pacific Ocean from France as part of the Louisiana Purchase. President Thomas Jefferson appointed his private secretary, Meriwether Lewis, to head an expedition across the Rocky Mountains to explore the Pacific Northwest. Lewis hired William Clark as his cocaptain, and the pair found forty-six men to travel with them on their journey. This team included artists, mapmakers, biologists, and other scientists. They studied and made note of plants, animals, minerals, and scenery along the way.

The Lewis and Clark expedition headed west from St. Louis, Missouri, in May 1804, travelling by canoe, on foot, and on horseback. After a grueling journey across the Rocky Mountains, the men paddled down the Columbia River, reaching the Pacific Ocean in November 1805.

A New Outpost

Lewis and Clark's men built a fort on the Pacific shore, near present-day Astoria, Oregon. They named it Fort Clatsop in honor of the local people who directed them to the spot. The fort was surrounded by lush ancient forests, wetlands, and wildlife. The explorers spent the cold, rainy winter trading tobacco and other goods with the Clatsop and drawing maps of the area. The Clatsop taught the explorers how to hunt, cure meat, and make moccasins and buckskin clothing using traditional Native American methods.

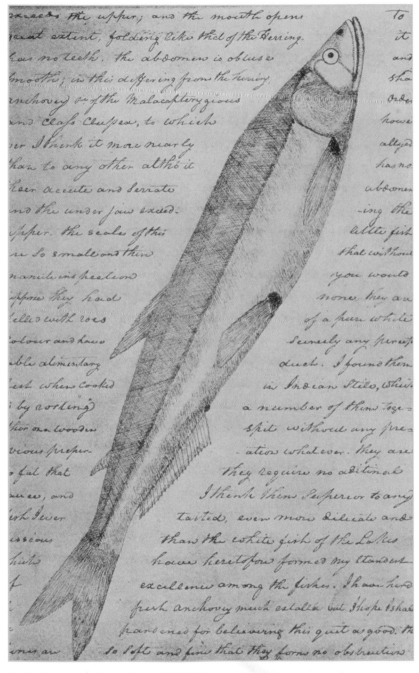

Meriwether Lewis and William Clark made notes and sketches of their discoveries as they explored the Pacific Northwest.

The Lewis and Clark expedition finally returned to St. Louis in September 1806. It was a complete success. Scientists who had been with the team were able to record volumes of information, proving that Oregon was rich with lumber, minerals, and fur-bearing animals.

Newspapers across the country printed news of the expedition. Hundreds of fur trappers, settlers, and explorers set out on foot to reap the wealth of the

When they reached Oregon's Pacific coast, Lewis and Clark's men built Fort Clatsop.

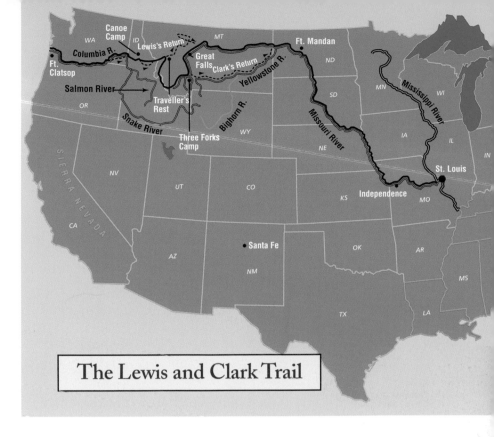

The Lewis and Clark Trail

West. Within a few years, thousands of Americans had sold their belongings and abandoned their lives in the East to follow in the footsteps of Lewis and Clark, hoping for a better life. A few of these people settled in Oregon, a place with riches found nowhere else on Earth.

Chapter Three

The Settlers

The first settlers in what would become the state of Oregon were fur trappers who moved there during the early nineteenth century. They were inspired by reports from the Lewis and Clark expedition that stated that the streams and rivers of Oregon were teeming with wildlife.

During the early nineteenth century, vast fortunes were made from the sale of beaver fur. Hats made from the pelts were extremely popular in both the United States and Europe. And all over the world, people prized clothing with fur collars, cuffs, and other decorations. Fur trappers could barely keep up with the demand for pelts from foxes, otters, panthers, bears, deer, and especially beavers. Fur-trading companies earned millions of dollars trading the pelts of more than 1 million animals every year.

The Fur Companies

By the beginning of the 1800s, several dozen American, Canadian, European, Chinese, and Russian fur traders settled in Oregon. Most of the fur trade was controlled by the Hudson Bay Company, a giant Canadian-based company owned by British citizens.

In 1811 John Jacob Astor, a wealthy New York businessman, challenged the Hudson Bay Company by starting his own fur-trading business, the Pacific Fur Company. Astor hired fur traders and sent them aboard the ship *Tonquin* to build a trading post south

Native Americans and Europeans trade furs for goods. Fur traders were Oregon's first settlers.

of the Columbia River. The trappers built four log huts, which they grandly named Fort Astoria in honor of Astor. From this post, trappers gathered furs from throughout the region and prepared them for shipping to Europe and China.

By 1812 war was brewing between Britain and America over control of the shipping trade. The British navy ruled the Pacific coast of Oregon. Workers at Fort Astoria feared that the British would seize the trading post when the War of 1812 began, so they sold it to the Hudson Bay Company. After the war ended in 1814, England and the United States agreed to share the area they called the Oregon Country, which included present-day Oregon, Washington, and Idaho. But the Hudson Bay Company continued to rule over all trading activity in the region.

The Life of a Trapper

The trappers who worked for the Hudson Bay Company led difficult lives in a dangerous environment. To capture beavers, trappers worked all day in freezing rivers, setting traps underwater to catch the water- loving animals. After several months of this back breaking labor, the trapper might come back to the fort with three or four hundred pelts. These could be sold for several thousand dollars total—a huge sum at a time when a skilled carpenter made about $1.50 a day.

There were many dangers for the trappers, who captured and killed animals in the forests and mountains as well as the rivers. Every year many trappers failed to return from the Oregon wilderness. Some

A fur trapper pauses at a river. The work of trappers was difficult, but they were able to earn thousands of dollars.

died in the woods due to accidents, starvation, or disease. Others were killed in fights with Native Americans or other trappers.

After selling their pelts, trappers took off a month or more to rest from their work. Groups of these mountain men gathered at campsites to spend their days drinking, gambling, and fighting.

The Father of Oregon

In 1821 Dr. John McLoughlin became head of the Oregon Country division of the Hudson Bay Company. McLoughlin was an educated man who believed in treating everyone fairly. He was on friendly terms

Dr. John McLoughlin, "the Father of Oregon," founded Oregon City as a haven for trappers.

with local Native Americans, many of whom worked for the Hudson Bay Company as trappers.

McLoughlin decided to help the American trappers who came to settle in the area, giving supplies to the ragged, hungry men who had traveled overland to settle in the Oregon Country. Because the Americans were competing with the British for control over the land and the fur trade, McLoughlin's unfriendly British bosses did not want him to help the starving American settlers.

Nevertheless, McLoughlin directed the American settlers, and most other newcomers, to a safe haven in the Willamette Valley. He eventually bought land and built his own house within the community he created there, which would be called Oregon City. In return, these grateful pioneers nicknamed McLoughlin "the Father of Oregon."

Missionaries

By the end of the 1820s, the days of fur trapping were coming to an end in Oregon as beavers were hunted to near extinction. Adventurous American farmers slowly began to move into the area, however, settling on lands that belonged to Native Americans. The British still believed that this land was part of Great Britain. To gain a foothold in the territory, the U.S. government encouraged American settlers to move to the region so the United States could officially claim the land.

In 1829 a movement called the American Society for Encouraging the Settlement of Oregon Territory began in Boston. At the same time, the group ran an advertisement in newspapers throughout the East claiming the Native Americans of Oregon wanted to become Christians. This group advertised for American **missionaries** to move west to Oregon in order to convert the Native Americans and populate the territory with U.S. citizens. It also raised money and bought supplies to lead a party of missionaries into the Willamette Valley.

The Willamette Valley was beautiful and fertile, and word of its bounty spread quickly to Americans in the East. More missionaries came, but by the late 1830s there were still fewer than one hundred American settlers in Oregon Country, more than half of them women and children. Oregon Country included present-day Oregon, Washington, Idaho, and parts of Wyoming, Montana, and Canada. The law required each area to have a population of sixty thousand American white male landowners to become a state.

Oregon City

As settlers continued to move slowly to Oregon, the United States fell into a deep economic depression.

A wagon train rolls through the Willamette Valley. The U.S. government encouraged Americans to settle in Oregon.

During the so-called Panic of 1837, banks failed, land and crop prices dropped, and people lost their farms in the eastern states. Some who lost everything were attracted to the promise of a fresh start on fertile land in the mild climate west of the Rocky Mountains.

In 1838 a missionary named Jason Lee rode from the Willamette Valley to the East Coast on horseback. He carried a **petition** to establish a U.S. territorial government. Along the way, he made more than seventy-five speeches about the rich soil and mild climate of the Willamette Valley. Lee's speeches interested settlers who were losing their farms in the East. He was able to recruit several educated men from the East to move to Oregon and help set up a government.

The Organic Act

In order to bring in more settlers and strengthen its claims to the land, the U.S. Congress enacted the Organic Act. The law granted 640 acres of land to every adult male settler and 160 acres per child. Before long the Organic Act attracted nearly one thousand settlers to the Oregon Country. They came in wagon trains along the Oregon Trail, a rutted path that stretched about two thousand miles from Independence, Missouri, to the Willamette Valley.

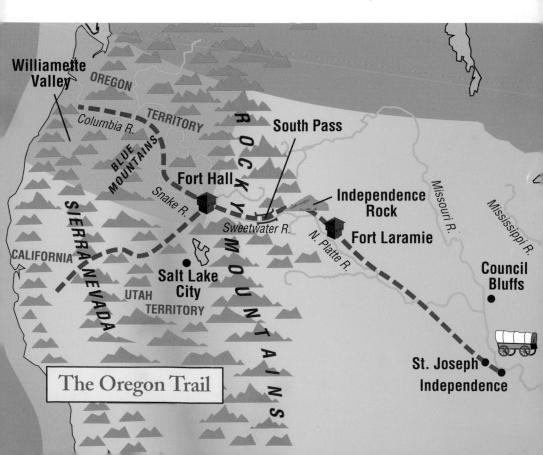

The Oregon Trail

Oregon

When the pioneers reached the end of the Oregon Trail, they found one of the most beautiful, fertile valleys in North America. A few staked their claims in present-day Oregon and built small farms, mostly in the Willamette Valley. Slowly they began to change the face of this ancient river valley while charting a new course for the Oregon Country.

Chapter Four

From Territory to State

In the early 1840s, the British navy controlled the Oregon coast and the British-owned Hudson Bay Company dominated the fur trade. But American officials insisted that the United States had a claim on the area since Lewis and Clark were the first to explore Oregon's interior. Americans also believed that John Jacob Astor had established rights to the area when he built Fort Astoria and other trading posts across the region during the 1810s.

Tensions continued to grow between the United States and Great Britain after thousands of Americans walked the Oregon Trail to the Willamette Valley. These excited people had heard about the free farmland available, and their rush to move to the valley became known as Oregon fever. Meanwhile, the

British grew alarmed as the trickle of American pioneers turned into a flood.

The British let the new arrivals live in peace, but many Americans began calling for war. These people demanded that Great Britain give up the entire Oregon Country—Oregon, Washington, and Idaho—to the United States.

Stepping over the Line

In the Willamette Valley, American settlers had tried to set up a government to strengthen their claim to the land. These people came from several different religious and political groups, however. When they tried to organize a government, they had trouble agreeing. In addition, the British and the French Canadian settlers in the area were not in favor of living under the U.S. government.

Then, in 1841, the pioneers came together in Salem to discuss a common enemy: the wolves. Where hungry wolves and fierce mountain lions roamed freely looking for food, the settlers were now raising large herds of cattle. And these cattle made quick and easy meals for the wild animals. One thing the pioneers could agree on was that the wolves and mountain lions had to be controlled.

At the first two wolf meetings, in February and March, the settlers agreed to pay taxes so a bounty could be paid to anybody who killed a wolf or a mountain lion. They also appointed a committee to consider creating a government to provide additional legal and military protections.

Pioneers in Oregon wanted to establish their own government, but British and French Canadian settlers voted against it.

At the third wolf meeting, held on on May 2, 1843, a committee of American settlers met at present-day Oregon City. These people were joined by British and French Canadians who were against creating an American government in the territory. When the vote was called, an American mountain man named Joseph Meeks drew a line in the dirt floor of the cabin. He asked those who wanted to establish an American government to step over.

Two of the French Canadians stepped over from the British side and joined the Americans, bringing the total to fifty two Americans and fifty British. These Americans and their French Canadian friends formed the first government and military force in the Pacific Northwest.

The Oregon Territory

The next year James Knox Polk was elected president of the United States. In his first speech as president, he rejected British claims on Oregon and said the Oregon Country belonged to the United States.

Even as the president gave his speech, Americans flooded into Oregon, about three thousand in 1844 alone. The new arrivals built farms and quickly founded towns such as Portland. The city grew so quickly that when trees were cut down to make streets, there was not enough time to remove the stumps. Portland

Settlers flooding into Oregon founded towns such as Portland, pictured here, which quickly became a bustling city.

is still known to locals by its old nickname of Stumptown.

In 1845 Oregonians elected their first temporary governor, George Abernethy. The next year Polk and Congress ended the agreement to share the territory with Great Britain and set the border of the United States at the southern edge of Alaska.

During the forceful, emotional discussions that followed between the two nations, the U.S. government sent the U.S. Navy ship *Shark* to secure the Oregon coast. The ship wrecked at the mouth of the Columbia River, however, and washed up near the old settlement left by Lewis and Clark. The huge gun from the ship washed ashore, giving the beach its name, Cannon Beach.

Finally, the British proposed the northern boundary of the United States in its present location, and the United States agreed to it. In 1846 the United States and Great Britain signed the Oregon Treaty, making present-day Oregon, Washington, and Idaho part of the United States. Congress named this area the Oregon Territory and asked Abraham Lincoln to be its first governor. Lincoln turned down the job, so Congress sent General Joseph Lane instead.

Gold Rush Settlers

In 1848 Oregon officially became a U.S. territory. Oregon City, the largest town in the territory, became the first capital. By then, about thirteen thousand settlers lived in Oregon, most of them around Oregon City.

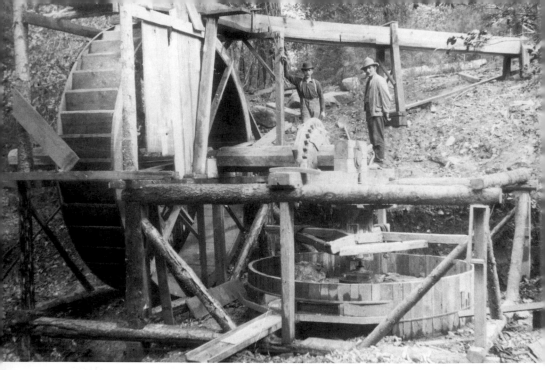

Miners pose for a photo at an Oregon gold mine. The discovery of gold in Oregon brought even more people to the area.

The California gold rush also started in 1848, and the gold fields south of Oregon were overrun by tens of thousands of people from all over the world. The large number of miners in California created a huge demand for food. This benefited Oregon farmers, who could now get top dollar for the crops shipped south to food stores in San Francisco.

Meanwhile, thousands of men who failed in the gold fields of California headed north looking for farmland. The government encouraged these men to stay with the Oregon Donation Land Act of 1850.

Under this new law, the government gave 320 acres of free land to any settler who farmed in Oregon for four years. Married men were given an extra 320 acres. This allowed each family to farm one square mile of land and encouraged a great land rush. As settlers poured in, they pressured the U.S. government to make Oregon a state.

The Changing Land

Native Americans watched with dismay as the exploding population changed the natural features of their ancient homeland. Not only did these settlers take lands that belonged to the tribes, but they drained wetlands used by birds and fish as well. They also built dikes to direct the water into their pastures and farmland. These actions drastically reduced the food supply, especially salmon, which were the main food source for most natives of Oregon.

Loggers pose next to giant felled trees. Settlers drastically changed the landscape of Oregon.

The U.S. government applied great pressure on the Native American people to give up their land and move to **reservations**. The tribes resisted because the reservations were in the most barren part of Oregon, where there was little water or wildlife to sustain people. To counter these fears, the government promised to provide food, education, and money to people who moved to reservations. Although some moved, these promises were never kept. People lived in dire poverty on the reservations, where disease and starvation ran rampant.

The Native American way of life that had thrived in Oregon for thousands of years was ending very quickly. In 1851 gold was discovered in Jackson Creek in southern Oregon, and an Oregon gold rush began. Soon people discovered more gold along the southern coast, at Pistol River, Gold Beach, and Port Orford.

Boomtowns sprang up in southwestern Oregon overnight. These rickety villages were collections of tents and log cabins set up very quickly by the men who came to dig for gold. Larger boomtowns, such as Jacksonville, included saloons and gambling houses lined up along the main street. In this rowdy atmosphere, fights often broke out between the miners and the remaining Native American population.

Statehood

Meanwhile, settlers continued to stream into the Oregon Territory, and small towns sprung up in Willamette Valley. In 1852 the territory's capital was moved to the town of Salem.

In 1853 Congress decided to divide the huge Oregon Territory into smaller territories. Congress divided off the Washington Territory to the north, creating Oregon's present border along the Columbia River.

On February 14, 1859, Oregon became the thirty-third state in the Union. Salem, in the beautiful Willamette Valley, became the new state capital. The people who moved to the Pacific coast, the lush forests, the towering Cascade mountains, and dramatic river valleys of Oregon were now proud citizens of the United States of America.

Facts About Oregon

State capital: Salem

Largest city: Portland

State motto: She Flies with Her Own Wings

State song: "Oregon, My Oregon"

State dance: square dance

State colors: navy blue and gold

State nickname: Beaver State

State flower: Oregon grape

State insect: Oregon swallowtail butterfly

State tree: Douglas fir

State nut: hazelnut (filbert)

State animal: beaver

State bird: western meadowlark

State fish: Chinook salmon

State rock: thunder egg (geode)

State gemstone: Oregon sunstone

Famous people: James Beard; Matt Groening; Mark Hatfield; Howard Hesseman; Chief Joseph; Kientpoos, who is also known as Captain Jack; Linus Pauling; Ahmad Rashad; Picabo Street; Sally Struthers

Glossary

barter: To trade goods or services without using money.

marsh: An area of soft, wet, grassy low-lying land, often forming between bodies of water and solid land.

missionary: One who is sent on a mission to do religious work in a territory or foreign country.

petition: An official written or printed paper requesting a right or benefit from a person or group in authority.

plateau: A high-level expanse of land; a tableland.

reservation: An area of land set apart by the federal government for the use of a Native American people.

For Further Exploration

Gretchen Bratvold, *Hello, U.S.A.: Oregon.* Minneapolis: Lerner, 1991. An introduction to the people, history, geography, and industry of Oregon. Includes famous people, facts at a glance, and a glossary.

Dennis Brindell Fradin and Judith Bloom Fradin, *From Sea to Shining Sea: Oregon.* Chicago: Childrens Press, 1995. An overview of Oregon's people, culture, history, economy, and government. Provides maps and lists of facts, descriptions of famous people, and a time line.

W. Scott Ingram, *Oregon.* New York: Childrens Press, 2000. This book describes the people, languages, religions, culture, sports, arts, geography, plants, animals, economy, and history of Oregon.

Rebecca Stefoff, *Celebrate the States: Oregon.* New York: Benchmark Books, 1997. An overview of the people, customs, history, and geography of Oregon. Contains lists of facts, famous people, state celebrations, and tourist sites.

Kathleen Thompson, *Portrait of America: Oregon.* Austin: Raintree Steck-Vaughn, 1996. Based on the *Portrait of America* television series, this book introduces the history, economy, and culture of Oregon. It includes a time line, facts, annual events, and places to visit.

For Further Exploration

Who Was Sacagawea? New York: Grosset & Dunlap, 2002. A short biography of Sacagawea, the Shoshone woman who helped the explorers Lewis and Clark on their expedition during the early 1800s.

Index

Index

Oregon

Picture Credits

Cover Photo: Private Collection/Bridgeman Art
  Library
© Bettmann/CORBIS, 36
© CORBIS, 37
© Hulton/Archive by Getty Images, 13, 15, 28
Chris Jouan, 8, 39
© The Newark Museum/Art Resource, NY, 11
© North Wind Picture Archives, 19, 23, 25, 33
Oregon Parks & Recreation Department/LCBO, 17
Oregon State Capitol, Legislative Administration, 26
© Joel W. Rogers/CORBIS, 14
With permission of the Royal Ontario Museum,
  © ROM, 7
© Lee Snider; Lee Snider/CORBIS, 20
© Stock Montage, Inc., 34

About the Authors

P. M. Boekhoff is the author of more than twenty-five nonfiction books for children. She has written about history, science, and the lives of creative people. In addition, P.M. Boekhoff is an artist who has created murals and theatrical scenics and has illustrated many book covers. In her spare time, she paints, draws, writes poetry, and studies herbal medicine.

Stuart A. Kallen is the author of more than 150 non-fiction books for children and young adults. He has written extensively about Native Americans and American history. In addition, Mr. Kallen has written award-winning children's videos and television scripts. In his spare time, Stuart A. Kallen is a singer/song-writer/guitarist in San Diego, California.